WITHDRAWN

Turtles

by Martha E. H. Rustad

Consulting Editor: Gail Saunders-Smith, Ph.D.

Consultant: Jennifer Zablotny, D.V.M.,
Member, American Animal Hospital Association

Pebble Books

an i...

Pebble Books are published by Capstone Press
151 Good Counsel Drive, P.O. Box 669, Mankato, Minnesota 56002
http://www.capstone-press.com

1 2 3 4 5 6 07 06 05 04 03 02

Library of Congress Cataloging-in-Publication Data
Rustad, Martha E. H. (Martha Elizabeth Hillman), 1975–
    Turtles / by Martha E. H. Rustad.
    p. cm.—(All about pets)
    Includes bibliographical references (p. 23) and index.
    ISBN 0-7368-0978-3
    1. Turtles as pets—Juvenile literature. [1. Turtles as pets. 2. Pets.] I. Title.
II. All about pets (Mankato, Minn.)
SF459.T8 R87 2002
639.3′92—dc21   2001000261

Summary: Simple text and photographs introduce and illustrate pet turtles, their
features, and care basics.

Note to Parents and Teachers

The All About Pets series supports national science standards
for units on the diversity and unity of life. This book describes
domesticated turtles and illustrates what they need from their
owners. The photographs support emergent readers in
understanding the text. The repetition of words and phrases
helps emergent readers learn new words. This book also introduces
emergent readers to subject-specific vocabulary words, which are
defined in the Words to Know section. Emergent readers may need
assistance to read some words and to use the Table of Contents,
Words to Know, Read More, Internet Sites, and Index/Word List
sections of the book.

Table of Contents

Some turtles are pets.

Turtles have a hard shell.

Turtles have soft skin.

tail

Turtles have a tail.

Some turtles swim.

14

Turtles need food
and water.

Turtles need a clean cage.

Turtles need room
to move.

Turtles need a place to hide.

Words to Know

cage—a container that holds an animal; a turtle needs a large cage or aquarium.

food—something that people, animals, and plants need to stay alive; each kind of turtle has a certain diet; turtles eat fruits, fish, vegetables, insects, and worms.

hide—to keep out of sight; some turtles like to hide most of the time.

pet—a tame animal kept for pleasure; only certain kinds of turtles should be kept as pets; wild turtles do not make good pets.

shell—a hard outer covering; turtles have a hard shell; most turtles can pull their head, feet, and tail into their shell for protection.

skin—the outer covering of tissue on the bodies of humans and animals

swim—to move through the water using the legs or tail; some turtles live in water most of the time; turtles need a dry place to rest.

Read More

Foley, Cate. *My Turtle.* My Pet. New York: Children's Press, 2000.

Gutman, Bill. *Becoming Best Friends with Your Iguana, Snake, or Turtle.* Pet Friends. Brookfield, Conn.: Millbrook Press, 2001.

Stone, Lynn M. *Box Turtles.* Unusual Pets. Vero Beach, Fla.: Rourke, 2001.

Internet Sites

Taking Care of Box Turtles
http://www.healthypet.com/Library/nutrition-7.html

Turtle and Tortoise Printouts
http://www.enchantedlearning.com/subjects/turtle/index.shtml

Turtle Times
http://www.turtletimes.com

Index/Word List

Word Count: 41
Early-Intervention Level: 6

Credits
Kia Bielke, cover designer and illustrator; Kimberly Danger, photo researcher

Capstone Press/Gary Sundermeyer, 4, 12, 16; Laurie Grassel, 14, 20
Photo Network/David Davis, 1; Karen Lawrence, 6
Pictor, cover, 18
Visuals Unlimited/Rob and Ann Simpson, 8; John D. Cunningham, 10

Special thanks to Pet Expo in Mankato, Minnesota, for their help with photo shoots
for this book. Turtles provided by Pet Expo, Mankato, Minnesota.